HEALTHY
Vegetarian

HEALTHY
Vegetarian

ANNIE NICHOLS

Photography by James Duncan

southwater

To my parents, Winnie and Fred, with thanks

This edition is published by Southwater

Southwater is an imprint of Anness Publishing Ltd
Hermes House, 88–89 Blackfriars Road, London SE1 8HA
tel. 020 7401 2077; fax 020 7633 9499
www.southwaterbooks.com; info@anness.com

© Anness Publishing Ltd 1994, 2001, 2006

UK agent: The Manning Partnership Ltd, 6 The Old Dairy,
Melcombe Road, Bath BA2 3LR; tel. 01225 478444;
fax 01225 478440; sales@manning-partnership.co.uk

UK distributor: Grantham Book Services Ltd, Isaac Newton Way,
Alma Park Industrial Estate, Grantham, Lincs NG31 9SD;
tel. 01476 541080; fax 01476 541061; orders@gbs.tbs-ltd.co.uk

North American agent/distributor: National Book Network,
4501 Forbes Boulevard, Suite 200, Lanham, MD 20706;
tel. 301 459 3366; fax 301 429 5746; www.nbnbooks.com

Australian agent/distributor: Pan Macmillan Australia, Level 18,
St Martins Tower, 31 Market St, Sydney, NSW 2000; tel. 1300 135
113; fax 1300 135 103; customer.service@macmillan.com.au

New Zealand agent/distributor: David Bateman Ltd,
30 Tarndale Grove, Off Bush Road, Albany, Auckland;
tel. (09) 415 7664; fax (09) 415 8892

Publisher: Joanna Lorenz
Series Editor: Lindsay Porter
Designer: Peter Laws
Photographer: James Duncan
Stylist: Madeleine Brehaut

Previously published as *Step-by-step 50 Quick and Healthy Vegetarian Dishes*

1 3 5 7 9 10 8 6 4 2

For all recipes, quantities are given in both metric and imperial
measures, and, where appropriate, measures are also given in
standard cups and spoons. Follow one set, but not a mixture,
because they are not interchangeable.

CONTENTS

INTRODUCTION

Vegetarianism is gaining an increasingly favourable image, and has come a long way from the heavy 'brown' food that was so prevalent over 20 years ago. These days the pressure is on to provide fresh, light, innovative ideas for the ever-increasing number of vegetarians. With the proliferation of new and exotic ingredients now available, exciting and imaginative dishes can be made with ease, drawing on a host of wonderful fresh produce and flavours.

A healthy vegetarian diet is easier to achieve than you might think. It is now generally accepted that about 50–70 per cent of our diet should be made up of foods rich in the complex carbohydrates that are found in cereals, grains, fruits and vegetables. These ingredients are naturally abundant in a well-balanced vegetarian diet and also have the advantage of being naturally low in fat. With the addition of nuts and pulses, they will provide sufficient protein to meet the body's requirements. If you include dairy foods in your vegetarian diet, moderate the consumption of those high in fat, and choose skimmed or semi-skimmed milk, low-fat yogurt and low- or medium-fat cheeses. Cheeses with a higher fat content, such as Parmesan, may be used in small amounts – as they are strong in flavour a little goes a long way. Control your use of oils, and choose unsaturated types such as olive, sunflower, corn or peanut. Using a non-stick frying pan will also help reduce the amount of fat used in cooking.

By combining a variety of different foods, a well-planned vegetarian diet will provide all the nutrients needed to maintain good health. This book contains dishes from all around the world, with something to suit every taste and occasion, proving that vegetarian food is both healthy, and anything but boring.

Fresh Fruit and Vegetables

Thanks to the amazing range of fresh produce now available, the vegetarian repertoire has expanded enormously. Filled with complex carbohydrates, protein, vitamins and minerals, fresh fruit and vegetables are essential to a healthy vegetarian diet.

Alfalfa sprouts
These crisp, sprouting seeds with a delicious nutty flavour are highly nutritious and rich in protein, fibre, vitamins and minerals.

Baby sweetcorn
These young corn are most delicious when lightly cooked, so are especially suitable for stir-fries.

Broad beans
The plump inner bean is delicious when lightly steamed, and makes a good accompaniment to richly flavoured foods.

Celeriac
This underrated vegetable has a delicious, sweet, celery-like flavour.

Chillies
There are hundreds of varieties of these hot relatives of the capsicum family. They should be treated with caution. When preparing chillies take special care to avoid rubbing your eyes or face as their juices can irritate the skin.

Fennel
A crisp, delicious, sweet aniseed-flavoured vegetable, which can be eaten raw, finely sliced, or cooked. Add a little to vegetable stock for an unusual extra flavouring.

Limes
Fresh and sharp with an intense sour flavour.

Okra
Okra lends a creamy, silky consistency to vegetable dishes.

Patty pan squash
These lovely, scallop-edged baby squash have a similar flavour to courgettes.

Peas
Sweet, tender peas, popped fresh from the pod are unbeatable. Make the most of them when in season.

Pumpkins
There are many different varieties of these members of the gourd family. A thick tough skin belies the fragrant, pale or bright orange flesh within.

Red onions
Mild and sweeter than most onions, their purple flesh makes a pretty addition to any vegetable dish.

Sweet potatoes
The skin of these tubers can be pinkish or brown and the flesh varies from creamy white to yellow or pale orange. Despite its name, this vegetable is not related to the everyday potato. The sweet potato usually has an elongated shape, although some round varieties are available.

Tomatoes
Recent demand for full-flavoured tomatoes means that varieties now abound, from the sweet little cherry tomatoes, to the plump Italian plum and the large beefsteak tomatoes.

Turnips
Sweet, nutty-flavoured turnips range from the walnut-sized baby roots (that are often sold still attached to their green tops) to large mature turnips.

fennel

okra

turnips

pumpkin

celeriac

tomatoes

chillies

plum tomatoes

broad beans

cherry tomatoes

sweet potatoes

peas

alfalfa sprouts

red onions

patty pan squash

limes

baby sweetcorn

Pasta, Pulses and Grains

Pasta, pulses and grains all belong to the important complex carbohydrate group. Most are low in fat and contain plenty of vitamins, minerals and dietary fibre.

Aduki beans
A small, reddish brown, shiny bean with a unique strong nutty, sweet flavour.

Arborio rice
One of the best and most commonly available rices to use for risotto.

Basmati rice and brown basmati rice
Harvested from the foothills of the Himalayas with a very distinctive, fragrant aroma.

Black-eyed beans
Sometimes referred to as black-eyed peas, these small beans with a black spot have a savoury flavour and succulent texture.

Bulgur wheat
A whole wheat grain that is steamed-dried and cracked so it only needs brief soaking before use.

Campanelle
A pretty frilled, twisted pasta tube.

Cannellini beans
These look like small white kidney beans and belong to the same family. They have a soft texture when cooked.

Capellini
Known as angel-hair pasta, this is a very fine variety.

Chick-peas
These pale golden-brown, hard peas look rather like small dry hazelnuts. They have a rich nutty flavour.

Couscous
Made from coarse semolina, this lovely soft grain is now produced to need only a brief moistening before use.

Egg noodles
The most common of all oriental noodles, they take only minutes to cook.

Flageolet beans
Pale green, long and slim, these are haricot beans removed from the pod while young. They have a tender texture when cooked.

Haricot beans
These oval cream beans are commonly seen as canned baked beans. A versatile bean with a mild flavour.

Long-grain rice and brown long-grain rice
Long, translucent grains are valued for their nutty flavour.

Oatmeal
Sliced whole oat grain which is graded from pinhead (the coarsest) to medium and fine (medium is shown here). A good source of calcium, potassium and iron.

Pasta bows
The Italian name for this is *farfalle* or 'butterfly', because of its shape.

Penne
Short, tubular pasta shapes, also known as quills.

Polenta
Fine yellow cornmeal, used to make a soft porridge of the same name.

Puy lentils
This superior lentil is prized for its flavour and texture.

Soup pasta
This tiny pasta comes in many different shapes.

Spaghetti
The most popular pasta, it has long, thin strands.

Tagliatelle
Flat, long ribbon noodles. The green version is flavoured with spinach.

Wild rice
Not a true rice but the seed of an aquatic grass. The brown, long grains open when cooked.

spaghetti

egg noodles

capellini

campanelle

tagliatelle

soup pasta

pasta bows

penne

arborio rice

wild rice

basmati rice

long-grain rice

brown long-grain rice

brown basmati rice

polenta

bulgur wheat

oatmeal

puy lentils

flageolet beans

cannellini beans

couscous

aduki beans

black-eyed beans

haricot beans

chick-peas

The Vegetarian Store Cupboard

Although not strictly essential, the ingredients listed here will greatly enhance any vegetarian dish, and are convenient to have on hand when preparing food at the last minute.

Balsamic vinegar
A deliciously smooth, rich, sweet-and-sour flavoured vinegar made in Modena in northern Italy.

Hazelnut oil
A richly flavoured nutty oil. Just a few drops will lift the flavour of a plain salad.

Olive oil
This is high in mono-unsaturated fats and vitamin A. It ranges from the refined pale yellow variety to the rich herbaceous extra-virgin.

Raspberry vinegar
A sweet, light vinegar with the slight tang of raspberries.

Sesame oil
This delicious, rich oil is often used in oriental cuisine as a flavouring rather than as a cooking oil.

Sunflower oil
A mild polyunsaturated oil that is useful for all types of cooking.

Sun-dried tomatoes
A preserved tomato which can be bought either in bags or steeped in olive oil in jars.

Tahini
A paste made from ground sesame seeds, it is widely used in Middle Eastern cooking.

Walnut oil
High in polyunsaturates, this is a delicious nutty oil.

raspberry vinegar

walnut oil

sunflower oil

balsamic vinegar

olive oil

sun-dried tomatoes

hazelnut oil

sesame oil

tahini

Herbs

Herbs can be used to enliven many dishes with aroma, flavour and colour. Use fresh herbs whenever possible.

dill

rosemary

marjoram

oregano

sage

bay leaf

tarragon

mint

thyme

Dill
A pungent, slightly sharp-tasting herb with anise overtones, used widely in Scandinavian, central and eastern-European cooking.

Flat-leaf parsley
More flavourful than the curly variety, this is a rich source of vitamins and minerals.

Marjoram
Very similar to oregano, though more delicate in flavour. Used widely in Italian cooking.

Mint
One of the most versatile of herbs, with a distinctive scent, mint is used in both sweet and savoury dishes.

Oregano
A wild variety of marjoram with a robust flavour.

Rosemary
Use this powerfully aromatic herb sparingly.

Sage
The aromatic oils in sage impart a distinct and powerful flavour, most often found in Italian cooking.

Sorrel
This fresh leafy herb has a sharp acidic flavour.

Tarragon
This has a sweet, spicy anise-like flavour.

Thyme
This robust aromatic herb is another vital ingredient of *bouquet garni*.

Basil
This herb has a rich, peppery, spicy smell and flavour, and has a perfect affinity with tomatoes.

Bay leaf
These glossy, dark green leaves are an essential ingredient of the classic *bouquet garni*.

Chervil
A delicate, feathery herb similar to parsley with a slightly sweet flavour reminiscent of anise.

Chives
This herb has a delicate oniony flavour.

Coriander
An intense, aromatic sweet and spicy herb.

coriander

chives

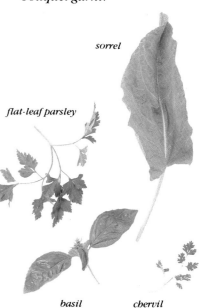

sorrel

flat-leaf parsley

basil   *chervil*

Spices and Seasonings

Spices and seasonings are indispensable for enhancing the flavours of foods that might otherwise be bland and lacking in substance.

fennel seeds

star anise

Allspice
This is available both whole and ground and imparts a flavouring that is like a mixture of nutmeg, cinnamon, cloves and pepper.

Caraway
A pungent and aromatic spice that is widely used in German and Austrian cooking.

Cayenne
Ground from small red chillies, it is extremely spicy, and should be used sparingly.

Cinnamon
Cinnamon is a sweet and fragrant spice ground from the dried, rolled inner bark of a tropical tree that is native to Sri Lanka.

Cloves
A strongly aromatic spice with a slightly bitter taste.

Coriander
A sweet, warm aromatic spice that is used extensively in Indian and South-east Asian cooking.

Cumin
A uniquely flavoured spice with a sweetly pungent and very distinctive taste.

Fennel seeds
These seeds have a strong, sweet anise-liquorice flavour.

Ginger
The fresh root has a clean refreshing flavour. Ginger is also available dried and ground.

Green cardamom
The pods should be broken open and the small black seeds ground to fully appreciate the mellow fragrant, slightly spicy aroma.

Juniper berries
These pine-scented, bitter-sweet berries provide the main flavouring of gin.

Lemon grass
A strong clean, refreshing citrus flavouring that is widely used in Thai and Vietnamese cooking.

Nutmeg
A very aromatic spice with a warm, sweet, nutty flavour.

Paprika
The flavour can range from sweet and lightly piquant, to pungent and fiery.

Saffron
This is the most expensive spice in the world, but you need only a tiny amount to flavour and colour any dish.

Star anise
A sweet, pungent liquorice-flavoured spice that is important in Chinese cooking.

Turmeric
Mainly used for its bright yellow colouring, it has a slightly musty taste and aroma.

Yellow mustard seeds
Less pungent than brown or black mustard seeds, they have a sweet, mild piquancy.

cayenne

ginger

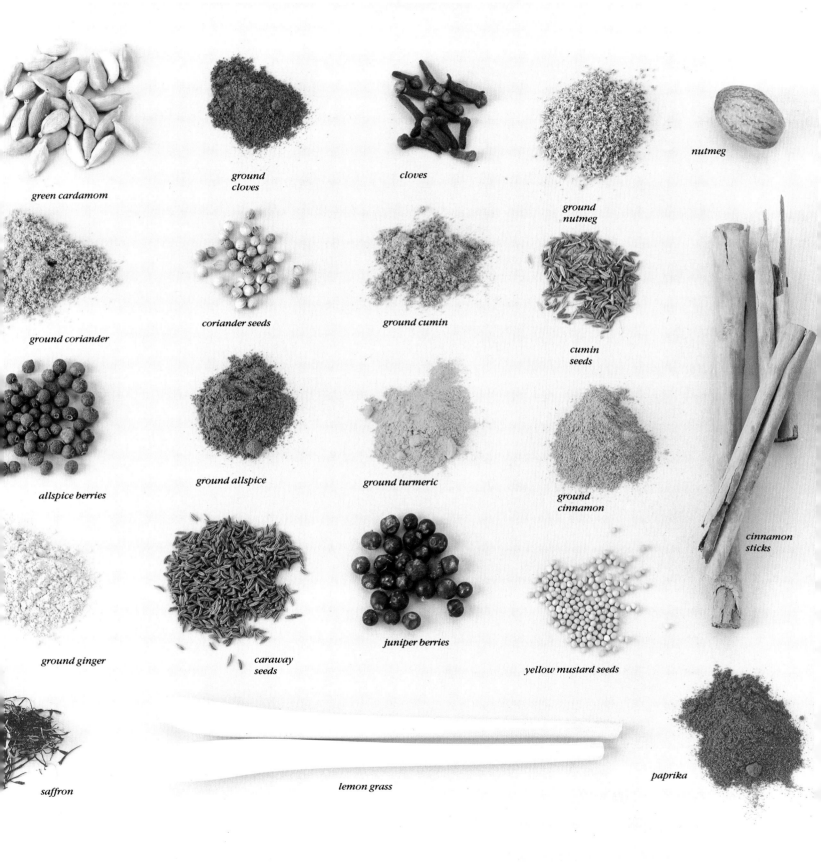

green cardamom

ground cloves

cloves

nutmeg

ground coriander

coriander seeds

ground cumin

ground nutmeg

cumin seeds

allspice berries

ground allspice

ground turmeric

ground cinnamon

ground ginger

caraway seeds

juniper berries

yellow mustard seeds

cinnamon sticks

saffron

lemon grass

paprika

Nuts

Nuts provide a healthy source of energy, and are rich in fibre, protein, vitamins B and E and several minerals. However, they are high in fats (though mostly mono- and polyunsaturated) so are usually also high in calories.

Almonds
There are two types, sweet and bitter, the bitter type being poisonous when eaten raw. This delicious nut enriches many dishes and is especially high in protein.

Brazil nuts
As the name would suggest, these nuts originate from the Brazilian Amazon. The high oil content means that these nuts quickly turn rancid.

Chestnuts
Not to be confused with the horse-chestnut, these softer textured nuts are low in fat and high in carbohydrates. They can be bought fresh, canned (whole or puréed), vacuum-packed and dried.

Hazelnuts
These wonderfully aromatic sweet nuts add flavour to both sweet and savoury dishes. Roasting adds more flavour.

Peanuts
Not strictly a true nut, these most popular of nuts have a distinctive flavour and are rich in protein.

Pecans
A native of the USA, these are sweet and richly flavoured nuts similar to walnuts.

Pine nuts
These soft, creamy coloured nuts are found at the base of a species of pine cone. They have a delicate flavour.

Pistachios
These are richly flavoured with a bright green colouring.

Walnuts
The most versatile of all nuts, walnuts impart a rich full flavour.

pecans

pistachios

chestnuts

brazil nuts

hazelnuts

peanuts

almonds

pine nuts

walnuts

Flours

Flour can be ground from grains, cereals, seeds, nuts and even roots and tubers.

Buckwheat flour
A non-wheat flour, ground from the seed of a plant that is related to rhubarb. It has a strong nutty flavour and is rich in vitamins A and B, calcium and carbohydrate.

White flour
This contains 75 per cent or less of the wheat grain so is not as nutritious as wholemeal flour.

Wholemeal flour
Ground from the entire whole grain it is rich in protein, vitamins and fibre, so is highly nutritious.

white flour

wholemeal flour

buckwheat flour

Seeds

Seeds provide a rich source of protein, fibre, vitamins, minerals and starch.

Poppy seeds
These mild, sweet seeds come from the opium poppy, but are free from narcotic properties.

Pumpkin seeds
From the vegetable of the same name, these flat green seeds have a light, distinctive flavour and are rich in zinc, protein and iron.

Sesame seeds
These tiny, light brown or creamy coloured seeds have a mild, sweet nutty flavour and are rich in protein and calcium.

Sunflower seeds
These seeds have a distinctive flavour and they are rich in protein, fibre, iron and calcium.

pumpkin seeds

poppy seeds

sunflower seeds

sesame seeds

TECHNIQUES

Once mastered, the techniques described here will help you to prepare vegetables speedily and with less waste, to produce better results with ease.

Peeling and Seeding Tomatoes

A simple and efficient way of preparing tomatoes.

1 Use a sharp knife to cut a small cross on the bottom of the tomato.

2 Turn the tomato over and cut out the core.

3 Immerse the tomato in boiling water for 10–15 seconds, then transfer to a bowl of cold water using a slotted spoon.

4 Lift out the tomato and peel (the skin should be easy to remove).

5 Cut the tomato in half crosswise and squeeze out the seeds.

6 Use a large knife to cut the peeled tomato into strips, then chop across the strips to make dice.

Chopping Onions

Uniform-sized dice make cooking easy. This method can't be beaten.

1 Peel the onion. Cut it in half with a large knife and set it cut-side down on a board. Make lengthwise vertical cuts along the onion, cutting almost but not quite through to the root.

2 Make 2 horizontal cuts from the stalk and towards the root, but not through it.

3 Cut the onion crosswise to form small, even dice.

Slicing Onions

Use thin slices for sautéeing or to flavour oils for stir-frying, or use sweet onion slices in salads.

1 Peel the onion. Cut it in half with a large knife and set it cut-side down on a chopping board.

2 Cut out a triangular piece of the core from each half.

3 Cut across each half in vertical slices.

Shredding Cabbage

This method is useful for coleslaws, pickled cabbage or any cooked dish.

1 Use a large knife to cut the cabbage into quarters.

2 Cut out the core from each quarter.

3 Slice across each quarter to form fine, even shreds.

Cutting Carrot Julienne

Thin julienne strips of any vegetable make decorative accompaniments, or can be used in stir-fries.

1 Peel the carrot and use a large knife to cut it into 5 cm/2 in lengths. Cut a thin sliver from one side of each piece so that it sits flat on the board.

2 Cut into thin lengthwise slices.

3 Stack the slices and cut through them to make fine strips.

Chopping Fresh Ginger

Fresh ginger imparts a clean, refreshing taste. Follow the instructions to chop finely.

1 Break off small knobs of ginger from the main root and peel.

2 Slice lengthwise and cut into strips.

3 Cut across the strips to form small, even dice.

Chopping Chillies

Fresh chillies must be handled with care. Always work in a well-ventilated area and keep away from your eyes.

1 Cut the chilli in half lengthwise and remove the core and seeds.

2 Cut it into lengthwise strips.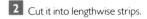

3 Cut across the strips to form small, even dice.

Melon and Basil Soups

A deliciously refreshing, chilled fruit soup, just right for a hot summer's day.

Serves 4–6

INGREDIENTS
2 Charentais or rock melons
75 g/3 oz/⅓ cup caster sugar
175 ml/6 fl oz/¾ cup water
finely grated rind and juice of 1 lime
45 ml/3 tbsp shredded fresh basil
fresh basil leaves, to garnish

basil

caster sugar

lime

Charentais melon

1 Cut the melons in half across the middle. Scrape out the seeds and discard. Using a melon baller, scoop out 20–24 balls and set aside for the garnish. Scoop out the remaining flesh and place in a blender or food processor.

2 Place the sugar, water and lime zest in a small pan over a low heat. Stir until dissolved, bring to the boil and simmer for 2–3 minutes. Remove from the heat and leave to cool slightly. Pour half the mixture into the blender or food processor with the melon flesh. Blend until smooth, adding the remaining syrup and lime juice to taste.

3 Pour the mixture into a bowl, stir in the basil and chill. Serve garnished with basil leaves and melon balls.

COOK'S TIP
Add the syrup in two stages, as the amount of sugar needed will depend on the sweetness of the melon.

Leek, Parsnip and Ginger Soup

A flavoursome winter warmer, with the added spiciness of fresh ginger.

Serves 4–6

INGREDIENTS
30 ml/2 tbsp olive oil
225 g/8 oz leeks, sliced
25 g/1 oz fresh ginger root, finely
    chopped
675 g/1½ lb parsnips, roughly
    chopped
300 ml/½ pint/1¼ cups dry white
    wine
1.1 litres/2 pints/5 cups vegetable
    stock or water
salt and freshly ground black pepper
low-fat fromage blanc, to garnish
paprika, to garnish

1 Heat the oil in a large pan and add the leeks and ginger. Cook gently for 2–3 minutes, until the leeks start to soften.

ginger

parsnips

vegetable stock

leek

2 Add the parsnips and cook for a further 7–8 minutes.

3 Pour in the wine and stock or water and bring to the boil. Reduce the heat and simmer for 20–30 minutes or until the parsnips are tender.

4 Purée in a blender until smooth. Season to taste. Reheat and garnish with a swirl of fromage blanc and a light dusting of paprika.

Chilled Fresh Tomato Soup

This effortless uncooked soup can be made in minutes.

Serves 4–6

INGREDIENTS
1.5 kg/3–3½ lb ripe tomatoes, peeled
   and roughly chopped
4 garlic cloves, crushed
30 ml/2 tbsp extra-virgin olive oil
   (optional)
30 ml/2 tbsp balsamic vinegar
freshly ground black pepper
4 slices wholemeal bread
low-fat fromage blanc, to garnish

wholemeal bread

garlic

fromage blanc

peppercorns

tomato

COOK'S TIP

For the best flavour, it is important to use only fully ripened, flavourful tomatoes in this soup.

1 Place the tomatoes in a blender with the garlic and olive oil if using. Blend until smooth.

2 Pass the mixture through a sieve to remove the seeds. Stir in the balsamic vinegar and season to taste with pepper. Leave in the fridge to chill.

3 Toast the bread lightly on both sides. Whilst still hot, cut off the crusts and slice in half horizontally. Place the toast on a board with the uncooked sides facing down and, using a circular motion, rub to remove any doughy pieces of bread.

4 Cut each slice into 4 triangles. Place on a grill pan and toast the uncooked sides until lightly golden. Garnish each bowl of soup with a spoonful of fromage blanc and serve with the melba toast.

Broccoli and Almond Soup

The creaminess of the toasted almonds combines perfectly with the slight bitterness of the taste of broccoli.

Serves 4–6

INGREDIENTS
50 g/2 oz/²⁄₃ cup ground almonds
675 g/1½ lb broccoli
850 ml/1½ pints/3¾ cups vegetable
   stock or water
300 ml/½ pint/1¼ cups skimmed
   milk
salt and freshly ground black pepper

ground almonds

skimmed milk

broccoli

1 Preheat the oven to 180°C/350°F/ Gas 4. Spread the ground almonds evenly on a baking sheet and toast in the oven for about 10 minutes, or until golden. Reserve ¼ of the almonds and set aside for the garnish.

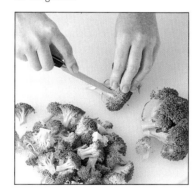

2 Cut the broccoli into small florets and steam for 6–7 minutes or until tender.

3 Place the remaining toasted almonds, broccoli, stock or water and milk in a blender and blend until smooth. Season to taste.

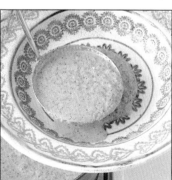

4 Reheat the soup and serve sprinkled with the reserved toasted almonds.

Red Onion and Beetroot Soup

This beautiful vivid ruby-red soup will look stunning at any dinner party.

Serves 4–6

INGREDIENTS
15 ml/1 tbsp olive oil
350 g/12 oz red onions, sliced
2 garlic cloves, crushed
275 g/10 oz cooked beetroot, cut into sticks
1.1 litres/2 pints/5 cups vegetable stock or water
50 g/2 oz/1 cup cooked soup pasta
30 ml/2 tbsp raspberry vinegar
salt and freshly ground black pepper
low-fat yogurt or fromage blanc, to garnish
snipped chives, to garnish

garlic

red onion

beetroot

pasta

chives

1 Heat the olive oil and add the onions and garlic.

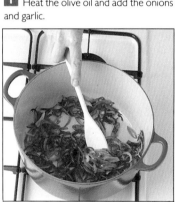

2 Cook gently for about 20 minutes or until soft and tender.

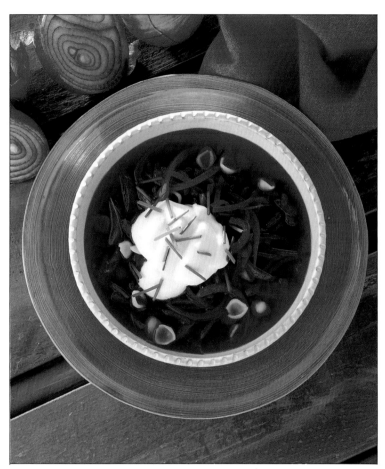

COOK'S TIP
Try substituting cooked barley for the pasta to give extra nuttiness.

3 Add the beetroot, stock or water, cooked pasta shapes and vinegar and heat through. Season to taste.

4 Ladle into bowls. Top each one with a spoonful of yogurt or fromage blanc and sprinkle with chives.

Cauliflower, Flageolet and Fennel Seed Soup

The sweet, anise-liquorice flavour of the fennel seeds gives a delicious edge to this hearty soup.

Serves 4–6

INGREDIENTS
15 ml/1 tbsp olive oil
1 garlic clove, crushed
1 onion, chopped
10 ml/2 tsp fennel seeds
1 cauliflower, cut into small florets
2 × 400 g/14 oz cans flageolet beans,
    drained and rinsed
1.1 litres/2 pints/5 cups vegetable
    stock or water
salt and freshly ground black pepper
chopped fresh parsley, to garnish
toasted slices of French bread, to
    serve

flageolet beans

French bread

onion

garlic

cauliflower

fennel seeds

parsley

1 Heat the olive oil. Add the garlic, onion and fennel seeds and cook gently for 5 minutes or until softened.

2 Add the cauliflower, half of the beans and the stock or water.

3 Bring to the boil. Reduce the heat and simmer for 10 minutes or until the cauliflower is tender.

4 Pour the soup into a blender and blend until smooth. Stir in the remaining beans and season to taste. Reheat and pour into bowls. Sprinkle with chopped parsley and serve with toasted slices of French bread.

Cucumber and Alfalfa Tortillas

Wheat tortillas are extremely simple to prepare at home. Served with a crisp, fresh salsa, they make a marvellous light lunch or supper dish.

COOK'S TIP

When peeling the avocado be sure to scrape off the bright green flesh from immediately under the skin as this gives the sauce its vivid green colour.

Serves 4

INGREDIENTS
225 g/8 oz/2 cups plain flour
pinch of salt
45 ml/3 tbsp olive oil
100 ml–150 ml/4–5 fl oz/½–⅔ cup
    warm water
lime wedges, to garnish

FOR THE SALSA
1 red onion, finely chopped
1 fresh red chilli, seeded and finely
    chopped
30 ml/2 tbsp chopped fresh dill or
    coriander
½ cucumber, peeled and chopped
175 g/6 oz alfalfa sprouts

FOR THE SAUCE
1 large avocado, peeled and stoned
juice of 1 lime
25 g/1 oz/2 tbsp soft goat's cheese
pinch of paprika

avocado

goat's cheese

red chilli

cucumber

dill   *alfalfa sprouts*

1 Mix all the salsa ingredients together in a bowl and set aside.

2 To make the sauce, place the avocado, lime juice and goat's cheese in a food processor or blender and blend until smooth. Place in a bowl and cover with clear film. Dust with paprika just before serving.

3 To make the tortillas, place the flour and salt in a food processor, add the oil and blend. Gradually add the water (the amount will vary depending on the type of flour). Stop adding water when a stiff dough has formed. Turn out onto a floured board and knead until smooth. Cover with a damp cloth.

4 Divide the mixture into 8 pieces. Knead each piece for a couple of minutes and form into a ball. Flatten and roll out each ball to a 23 cm/9 in circle.

5 Heat an ungreased heavy-based pan. Cook 1 tortilla at a time for about 30 seconds on each side. Place the cooked tortillas in a clean tea-towel and repeat until you have 8 tortillas.

6 To serve, spread each tortilla with a spoonful of avocado sauce, top with salsa and roll up. Garnish with lime wedges.

Baked Herb Crêpes

These mouth-watering, light herb crêpes make a striking starter at a dinner party, but are equally splendid served with a crisp salad for lunch.

Serves 4

INGREDIENTS
25 g/1 oz chopped fresh herbs
  (e.g. parsley, thyme, and chervil)
15 ml/1 tbsp sunflower oil, plus extra
  for frying
100 ml/4 fl oz/½ cup skimmed milk
3 × size 3 eggs
25 g/1 oz/¼ cup plain flour
pinch of salt

FOR THE SAUCE
30 ml/2 tbsp olive oil
1 small onion, chopped
2 garlic cloves, crushed
15 ml/1 tbsp grated fresh ginger root
1 × 400 g/14 oz can chopped
  tomatoes

FOR THE FILLING
450 g/1 lb fresh spinach
175 g/6 oz/¾ cup ricotta cheese
25 g/1 oz/2 tbsp pine nuts, toasted
5 halves sun-dried tomatoes in olive
  oil, drained and chopped
30 ml/2 tbsp shredded fresh basil
salt, nutmeg and freshly ground black
  pepper
4 egg whites

2 Heat a small non-stick crêpe or frying pan and add a very small amount of oil. Pour out any excess oil and pour in a ladleful of the batter. Swirl around to cover the base. Cook for 1–2 minutes, turn over and cook the other side. Repeat to make 8 crêpes.

3 To make the sauce, heat the oil in a small pan. Add the onion, garlic and ginger and cook gently for 5 minutes until softened. Add the tomatoes and cook for a further 10–15 minutes until the mixture thickens. Purée, sieve and set aside.

1 To make the crêpes, place the herbs and oil in a blender and blend until smooth, pushing down any whole pieces with a spatula. Add the milk, eggs, flour and salt and process again until smooth and pale green. Leave to rest for 30 minutes.

onion

parsley

ginger

*chopped
tomatoes*

spinach

*sun-dried
tomatoes*

garlic

nutmeg

thyme

flour

egg

skimmed milk

4 To make the filling, wash the spinach, removing any large stalks, and place in a large pan with only the water that clings to the leaves. Cover and cook, stirring once, until the spinach has just wilted. Remove from the heat and refresh in cold water. Place in a sieve or colander, squeeze out the excess water and chop finely. Mix the spinach with the ricotta, pine nuts, sun-dried tomatoes and basil. Season with salt, nutmeg and freshly ground black pepper.

5 Preheat the oven to 190°C/375°F/ Gas 5. Whisk the 4 egg whites until stiff but not dry. Fold ⅓ into the spinach and ricotta to lighten the mixture, then gently fold in the rest.

6 Taking each crêpe at a time, place on a lightly oiled baking sheet. Place a large spoonful of filling on each one and fold into quarters. Repeat until all the filling and crêpes are used up. Bake in the oven for 10–15 minutes or until set. Reheat the tomato sauce to serve with the crêpes.

COOK'S TIP

If preferred, use plain sun-dried tomatoes without any oil, and soak them in warm water for 20 minutes before using.

Buckwheat Blinis

These delectable light pancakes originated in Russia. For a special occasion, serve with a small glass of chilled vodka.

Serves 4

INGREDIENTS
5 ml/1 tsp easy-blend dry yeast
250 ml/8 fl oz/1 cup skimmed milk, warmed
40 g/1½ oz/⅓ cup buckwheat flour
40 g/1½ oz/⅓ cup plain flour
10ml/2 tsp caster sugar
pinch of salt
1 × size 3 egg, separated
oil, for frying

FOR THE AVOCADO CREAM
1 large avocado
75 g/3 oz/⅓ cup low-fat fromage blanc
juice of 1 lime

FOR THE PICKLED BEETROOT
225 g/8 oz beetroot
45 ml/3 tbsp lime juice
snipped chives, to garnish
cracked black peppercorns, to garnish

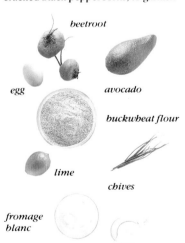

beetroot

egg

avocado

buckwheat flour

lime

chives

fromage blanc

skimmed milk

1 Mix the dry yeast with the milk, then mix with the next 4 ingredients and the egg yolk. Cover with a cloth and leave to prove for about 40 minutes. Whisk the egg white until stiff but not dry and fold into the blini mixture.

2 Heat a little oil in a non-stick pan and add a ladleful of batter to make a 10 cm/ 4 in pancake. Cook for 2–3 minutes on each side. Repeat with the remaining batter mixture to make 8 blinis.

3 Cut the avocado in half and remove the stone. Peel and place the flesh in a blender with the fromage blanc and lime juice. Blend until smooth.

4 Peel the beetroot and shred finely. Mix with the lime juice. To serve, top each blini with a spoonful of avocado cream. Serve with the pickled beetroot and garnish with snipped chives and cracked black peppercorns.

Cheese-stuffed Pears

These pears, with their scrumptious creamy topping, make a sublime dish when served with a simple salad.

Serves 4

INGREDIENTS

50 g/2 oz/¼ cup ricotta cheese
50 g/2 oz/¼ cup dolcelatte cheese
15 ml/1 tbsp honey
½ celery stick, finely sliced
8 green olives, pitted and roughly
  chopped
4 dates, stoned and cut into thin strips
pinch of paprika
4 ripe pears
150 ml/¼ pint/⅔ cup apple juice

honey

pear

apple juice

dates

dolcelatte

celery

olives

1 Preheat the oven to 200°C/400°F/ Gas 6. Place the ricotta in a bowl and crumble in the dolcelatte. Add the rest of the ingredients except for the pears and apple juice and mix well.

2 Halve the pears lengthwise and use a melon baller to remove the cores. Place in a ovenproof dish and divide the filling equally between them.

3 Pour in the apple juice and cover the dish with foil. Bake for 20 minutes or until the pears are tender.

4 Remove the foil and place the dish under a hot grill for 3 minutes. Serve immediately.

COOK'S TIP

Choose ripe pears in season such as Conference, William or Comice.

Soufflé Omelette

This delectable soufflé omlette is light and delicate enough to melt in the mouth.

Serves 1

INGREDIENTS
2 eggs, separated
30 ml/2 tbsp cold water
15 ml/1 tbsp chopped fresh coriander
salt and freshly ground black pepper
7.5 ml/½ tbsp olive oil
30 ml/2 tbsp mango chutney
25 g/1 oz/¼ cup Jarlsberg cheese, grated

Jarlsberg

mango chutney

eggs

coriander

COOK'S TIP

A light hand is essential to the success of this dish. Do not overmix the egg whites into the yolks or the mixture will be heavy.

1 Beat the egg yolks together with the cold water, coriander and seasoning.

2 Whisk the egg whites until stiff but not dry and gently fold into the egg yolk mixture.

3 Heat the oil in a frying pan, pour in the egg mixture and reduce the heat. Do not stir. Cook until the omelette becomes puffy and golden brown on the underside (carefully lift one edge with a palette knife to check).

4 Spoon on the chutney and sprinkle on the Jarlsberg. Fold over and slide onto a warm plate. Eat immediately. (If preferred, before adding the chutney and cheese, place the pan under a hot grill to set the top.)

Nutty Cheese Balls

An extremely quick and simple recipe. Try making a smaller version to serve as canapés at a drinks party.

Serves 4

INGREDIENTS
225 g/8 oz/1 cup low-fat soft cheese
   such as Quark
50 g/2 oz/¼ cup dolcelatte cheese
15 ml/1 tbsp finely chopped onion
15 ml/1 tbsp finely chopped celery
   stick
15 ml/1 tbsp finely chopped parsley
15 ml/1 tbsp finely chopped gherkin
5 ml/1 tsp brandy or port (optional)
pinch of paprika
50 g/2 oz/½ cup walnuts, roughly
   chopped
90 ml/6 tbsp snipped chives
salt and freshly ground black pepper

celery

dolcelatte

gherkins

soft cheese

onion

walnuts

chives

parsley

paprika

1 Beat the soft cheese and dolcelatte together using a spoon.

2 Mix in all the remaining ingredients, except the snipped chives.

3 Divide the mixture into 12 pieces and roll into balls.

4 Roll each ball gently in the snipped chives. Leave in the fridge to chill for about an hour before serving.

Sweet Potato Roulade

Sweet potato works particularly well as the base for this roulade. Serve in thin slices for a truly impressive dinner party dish.

Serves 6

INGREDIENTS

225 g/8 oz/1 cup low-fat soft cheese
   such as Quark
75 ml/5 tbsp low-fat yogurt
6–8 spring onions, finely sliced
30 ml/2 tbsp chopped brazil nuts,
   roasted
450 g/1 lb sweet potatoes, peeled and
   cubed
12 allspice berries, crushed
4 eggs, separated
50 g/2 oz/¼ cup Edam cheese, finely
   grated
salt and freshly ground black pepper
15 ml/1 tbsp sesame seeds

soft cheese

sesame seeds

sweet potato

yogurt

Edam

brazil nuts

spring onions

egg

peppercorns

1 Preheat the oven to 200°C/400°F/Gas 6. Grease and line a 33 × 25 cm/13 × 10 in Swiss roll tin with non-stick baking paper, snipping the corners with scissors to fit.

2 In a small bowl, mix together the soft cheese, yogurt, spring onions and brazil nuts. Set aside.

3 Boil or steam the sweet potato until tender. Drain well. Place in a food processor with the allspice and blend until smooth. Spoon into a bowl and stir in the egg yolks and Edam. Season to taste.

4 Whisk the egg whites until stiff but not dry. Fold ⅓ of the egg whites into the sweet potatoes to lighten the mixture before gently folding in the rest.

5 Pour into the prepared tin, tipping it to get the mixture right into the corners. Smooth gently with a palette knife and cook in the oven for 10–15 minutes.

COOK'S TIP
Choose the orange-fleshed variety of sweet potato for the most striking colour.

6 Meanwhile, lay a large sheet of greaseproof paper on a clean tea-towel and sprinkle with the sesame seeds. When the roulade is cooked, tip it onto the paper, trim the edges and roll it up. Leave to cool. When cool carefully unroll, spread with the filling and roll up again. Cut into slices to serve.

Pumpkin and Pistachio Risotto

This elegant combination of creamy golden rice and orange pumpkin can be as pale or bright as you like by adding different quantities of saffron.

Serves 4

INGREDIENTS
1.1 litres/2 pints/5 cups vegetable
    stock or water
generous pinch of saffron threads
30 ml/2 tbsp olive oil
1 medium onion, chopped
2 garlic cloves, crushed
450 g/1 lb arborio rice
900 g/2 lb pumpkin, peeled, seeded
    and cut into 2 cm/¾ in cubes
200 ml/7 fl oz/¾ cup dry white wine
15 g/½ oz Parmesan cheese, finely
    grated
50 g/2 oz/½ cup pistachios
45 ml/3 tbsp chopped fresh marjoram
    or oregano, plus extra leaves, to
    garnish
salt, freshly grated nutmeg and ground
    black pepper

saffron

pumpkin

white wine

onion

garlic

marjoram

Parmesan

arborio rice

pistachios

1 Bring the stock or water to the boil and reduce to a low simmer. Ladle a little stock into a small bowl. Add the saffron threads and leave to infuse.

4 Gradually add the stock or water, a ladleful at a time, allowing the rice to absorb the liquid before adding more and stirring all the time. After 20–30 minutes the rice should be golden yellow and creamy, and *al dente* when tested.

2 Heat the oil in a large saucepan. Add the onion and garlic and cook gently for about 5 minutes until softened. Add the rice and pumpkin and cook for a few more minutes until the rice looks transparent.

3 Pour in the wine and allow it to bubble hard. When it is absorbed add ¼ of the stock and the infused saffron and liquid. Stir constantly until all the liquid is absorbed.

5 Stir in the Parmesan cheese, cover the pan and leave to stand for 5 minutes.

6 To finish, stir in the pistachios and marjoram or oregano. Season to taste with a little salt, nutmeg and pepper, and scatter over a few extra marjoram or oregano leaves.

COOK'S TIP
Italian arborio rice must be used to make an authentic risotto. Choose unpolished white arborio as it contains more starch.

Wild Rice Rösti with Carrot and Orange Purée

Rösti is a traditional dish from Switzerland. This variation has the extra nuttiness of wild rice and a bright simple sauce as a fresh accompaniment.

Serves 6

INGREDIENTS
50 g/2 oz/½ cup wild rice
900 g/2 lb large potatoes
45 ml/3 tbsp walnut oil
5 ml/1 tsp yellow mustard seeds
1 onion, coarsely grated and drained
  in a sieve
30 ml/2 tbsp fresh thyme leaves
salt and freshly ground black pepper

FOR THE PURÉE
350 g/12 oz carrots, peeled and
  roughly chopped
rind and juice of 1 large orange

onion

thyme

carrot

wild rice

potatoes

yellow mustard seeds

orange

1 For the purée, place the carrots in a pan, cover with cold water and add 2 pieces of orange rind. Bring to the boil and cook for 10 minutes or until tender. Drain well and discard the rind.

2 Purée the mixture in a blender with 60 ml/4 tbsp of the orange juice. Return to the pan to reheat.

3 Place the wild rice in a clean pan and cover with water. Bring to the boil and cook for 30–40 minutes, until the rice is just starting to split, but still crunchy. Drain the rice.

4 Scrub the potatoes, place in a large pan and cover with cold water. Bring to the boil and cook for 10–15 minutes until just tender. Drain well and leave to cool slightly. When the potatoes are cool, peel and coarsely grate them into a large bowl. Add the cooked rice.

5 Heat 30 ml/2 tbsp of the walnut oil in a non-stick frying pan and add the mustard seeds. When they start to pop, add the onion and cook gently for 5 minutes until softened. Add to the bowl of potato and rice, together with the thyme, and mix thoroughly. Season to taste with salt and pepper.

6 Heat the remaining oil in the frying pan and add the potato mixture. Press down well and cook for 10 minutes or until golden brown. Cover the pan with a plate and flip over, then slide the rösti back into the pan for another 10 minutes to cook the other side. Serve with the reheated carrot and orange purée.

Thai Fragrant Rice

A lovely, soft, fluffy rice dish, perfumed with fresh lemon grass.

Serves 4

INGREDIENTS
1 piece of lemon grass
2 limes
225 g/8 oz/1 cup brown basmati rice
15 ml/1 tbsp olive oil
1 onion, chopped
2.5 cm/1 in piece of fresh ginger root,
   peeled and finely chopped
7.5 ml/1½ tsp coriander seeds
7.5 ml/1½ tsp cumin seeds
700 ml/1¼ pints/3 cups vegetable
   stock
60 ml/4 tbsp chopped fresh coriander
lime wedges, to serve

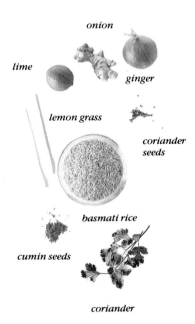

onion

lime

ginger

lemon grass

coriander seeds

basmati rice

cumin seeds

coriander

1 Finely chop the lemon grass.

2 Remove the zest from the limes using a zester or fine grater.

3 Rinse the rice in plenty of cold water until the water runs clear. Drain through a sieve.

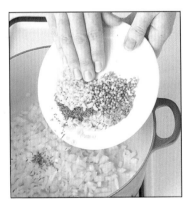

4 Heat the oil in a large pan and add the onion, spices, lemon grass and lime zest and cook gently for 2–3 minutes.

5 Add the rice and cook for another minute, then add the stock and bring to the boil. Reduce the heat to very low and cover the pan. Cook gently for 30 minutes then check the rice. If it is still crunchy, cover the pan again and leave for a further 3–5 minutes. Remove from the heat.

6 Stir in the fresh coriander, fluff up the grains, cover and leave for 10 minutes. Serve with lime wedges.

COOK'S TIP

Other varieties of rice, such as white basmati or long grain, can be used for this dish but you will need to adjust the cooking times accordingly.

Cannellini Bean Pureé with Grilled Radicchio

The slightly bitter flavours of the radicchio and chicory make a wonderful marriage with the creamy citrus bean purée.

Serves 4

INGREDIENTS
1 × 400 g/14 oz can cannellini beans
45 ml/3 tbsp low-fat fromage blanc
finely grated zest, rind and juice of 1
  large orange
15 ml/1 tbsp finely chopped fresh
  rosemary
4 heads of chicory
2 medium radicchio
15 ml/1 tbsp walnut oil

chicory

fromage blanc

cannellini beans

rosemary

raddichio

orange

1 Drain the beans, rinse, and drain again. Purée the beans in a blender or food processor with the fromage blanc, orange zest, orange juice and rosemary. Set aside.

2 Cut the chicory in half lengthwise.

3 Cut each radicchio into 8 wedges

4 Lay out the chicory and radicchio on a baking tray and brush with walnut oil. Grill for 2–3 minutes. Serve with the puree and scatter over the orange rind.

COOK'S TIP
Other suitable beans to use are haricot, mung or broad beans.

Tabbouleh with Fennel and Pomegranate

A fresh salad originating in the Middle East, with the added crunchiness of fennel and sweet pomegranate seeds. It is perfect for a summer lunch.

Serves 6

INGREDIENTS

225 g/8 oz/1 cup bulgur wheat
2 fennel bulbs
1 small fresh red chilli, seeded and
    finely chopped
1 celery stick, finely sliced
30 ml/2 tbsp olive oil
finely grated rind and juice of 2
    lemons
6–8 spring onions, chopped
90 ml/6 tbsp chopped fresh mint
90 ml/6 tbsp chopped fresh parsley
1 pomegranate, seeds removed
salt and freshly ground black pepper

1 Place the bulgur wheat in a bowl and pour over enough cold water to cover. Leave to stand for 30 minutes.

lemon

red chilli

celery

bulgur wheat

spring onion

fennel

pomegranate   parsley   mint

2 Drain the wheat through a sieve, pressing out any excess water using a spoon.

3 Halve the fennel bulbs and cut into very fine slices.

4 Mix all the remaining ingredients together, including the soaked bulgur wheat and fennel. Season well, cover, and set aside for 30 minutes before serving.

Sweet Vegetable Couscous

A wonderful combination of sweet vegetables and spices, this makes a substantial winter dish.

Serves 4–6

INGREDIENTS
1 generous pinch of saffron threads
45 ml/3 tbsp boiling water
15 ml/1 tbsp olive oil
1 red onion, sliced
2 garlic cloves crushed
1–2 fresh red chillies, seeded and
  finely chopped
2.5 ml/½ tsp ground ginger
2.5 ml/½ tsp ground cinnamon
1 × 400 g/14 oz can chopped
  tomatoes
300 ml/½ pint/1¼ cups vegetable
  stock or water
4 medium carrots, peeled and cut into
  5 mm/¼ in slices
2 medium turnips, peeled and cut into
  2 cm/¾ in cubes
450 g/1 lb sweet potatoes, peeled and
  cut into 2 cm/¾ in cubes
75 g/3 oz/⅓ cup raisins
2 medium courgettes, cut into 5 mm/
  ¼ in slices
1 × 400 g/14 oz can chick-peas,
  drained and rinsed
45 ml/3 tbsp chopped fresh parsley
45 ml/3 tbsp chopped fresh coriander
450 g/1 lb quick-cook couscous

1 Leave the saffron to infuse in the boiling water.

2 Heat the oil in a large saucepan. Add the onion, garlic and chillies and cook gently for 5 minutes.

3 Add the ground ginger and cinnamon and cook for a further 1–2 minutes.

4 Add the tomatoes, stock or water, infused saffron and liquid, carrots, turnips, sweet potatoes and raisins, cover and simmer for 25 minutes.

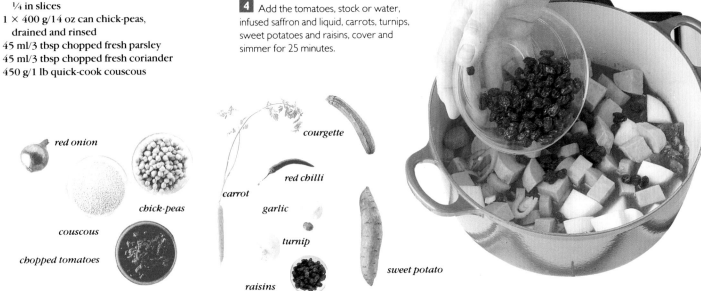

red onion

courgette

red chilli

carrot

garlic

chick-peas

couscous

turnip

chopped tomatoes

sweet potato

raisins

5 Add the courgettes, chick-peas, parsley and coriander and cook for another 10 minutes.

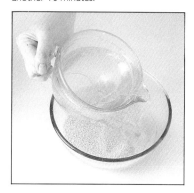

6 Meanwhile prepare the couscous following the packet instructions and serve with the vegetables.

Lemon and Ginger Spicy Beans

An extremely quick delicious meal, made with canned beans for speed. You probably won't need extra salt as canned beans tend to be already salted.

Serves 4

INGREDIENTS

5 cm/2 in piece fresh ginger root, peeled and roughly chopped
3 garlic cloves, roughly chopped
250 ml/8 fl oz/1 cup cold water
15 ml/1 tbsp sunflower oil
1 large onion, thinly sliced
1 fresh red chilli, seeded and finely chopped
¼ tsp cayenne pepper
10 ml/2 tsp ground cumin
5 ml/1 tsp ground coriander
½ tsp ground turmeric
30 ml/2 tbsp lemon juice
75 g/3 oz/⅓ cup chopped fresh coriander
1 × 400 g/14 oz can black-eyed beans, drained and rinsed
1 × 400 g/14 oz can aduki beans, drained and rinsed
1 × 400 g/14 oz can haricot beans, drained and rinsed
freshly ground black pepper

1 Place the ginger, garlic and 60 ml/4 tbsp of the cold water in a blender and mix until smooth.

2 Heat the oil in a pan. Add the onion and chilli and cook gently for 5 minutes until softened.

3 Add the cayenne pepper, cumin, ground coriander and turmeric and stir-fry for 1 minute.

4 Stir in the ginger and garlic paste from the blender and cook for another minute.

garlic

red chilli

aduki beans

ginger

ground coriander

black-eyed beans

ground turmeric

ground cumin

haricot beans

onion

5 Add the remaining water, lemon juice and fresh coriander, stir well and bring to the boil. Cover the pan tightly and cook for 5 minutes.

6 Add all the beans and cook for a further 5–10 minutes. Season with pepper and serve.

Green Lentil and Cabbage Salad

This warm crunchy salad makes a satisfying meal if served with crusty French bread or wholemeal rolls.

Serves 4–6

INGREDIENTS
225 g/8 oz/1 cup puy lentils
1.3 litres/2¼ pints/6 cups cold water
1 garlic clove
1 bay leaf
1 small onion, peeled and studded
    with 2 cloves
15 ml/1 tbsp olive oil
1 red onion, finely sliced
2 garlic cloves, crushed
15 ml/1 tbsp thyme leaves
350 g/12 oz cabbage, finely shredded
finely grated rind and juice of 1 lemon
15 ml/1 tbsp raspberry vinegar
salt and freshly ground black pepper

thyme

cabbage

onion

red onion

bay leaf

lemon

garlic

cloves

peppercorns

1 Rinse the lentils in cold water and place in a large pan with the water, peeled garlic clove, bay leaf and clove-studded onion. Bring to the boil and cook for 10 minutes. Reduce the heat, cover the pan and simmer gently for 15–20 minutes. Drain and remove the onion, garlic and bay leaf.

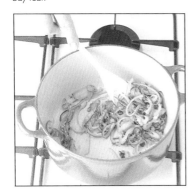

2 Heat the oil in a large pan. Add the red onion, garlic and thyme and cook for 5 minutes until softened.

3 Add the cabbage and cook for 3–5 minutes until just cooked but still crunchy.

4 Stir in the cooked lentils, lemon rind and juice and the raspberry vinegar. Season to taste and serve.

Polenta and Baked Tomatoes

A staple of northern Italy, polenta is a nourishing, filling food, served here with a delicious fresh tomato and olive topping.

Serves 4–6

INGREDIENTS
2 litres/3½ pints/9 cups water
500 g/1¼ lb quick-cook polenta
12 large ripe plum tomatoes, sliced
4 garlic cloves, thinly sliced
30 ml/2 tbsp chopped fresh oregano
  or marjoram
115 g/4 oz/½ cup black olives, pitted
salt and freshly ground black pepper
30 ml/2 tbsp olive oil

black olives

marjoram

plum tomatoes

garlic

oregano

polenta

1 Place the water in a large saucepan and bring to the boil. Whisk in the polenta and simmer for 5 minutes.

2 Remove the pan from the heat and pour the polenta into a 23 cm × 33 cm/ 9 in × 13 in Swiss roll tin. Smooth out the surface with a palette knife until level, and leave to cool.

3 Preheat the oven to 180°C/350°F/ Gas 4. With a 7.5 cm/3 in round pastry cutter, stamp out 12 rounds of polenta. Lay them so that they slightly overlap in a lightly oiled ovenproof dish.

4 Layer the tomatoes, garlic, oregano or marjoram and olives on top of the polenta, seasoning the layers as you go. Sprinkle with the olive oil, and bake uncovered for 30–35 minutes. Serve immediately.

PASTA AND NOODLES

Sesame Noodle Salad with Hot Peanuts

An orient-inspired salad with crunchy vegetables and a light soy dressing. The hot peanuts make a surprisingly successful union with the cold noodles.

Serves 4

INGREDIENTS
350 g/12 oz egg noodles
2 carrots, peeled and cut into fine julienne strips
½ cucumber, peeled and cut into 1 cm/½ in cubes
115 g/4 oz celeriac, peeled and cut into fine julienne strips
6 spring onions, finely sliced
8 canned water chestnuts, drained and finely sliced
175 g/6 oz beansprouts
1 small fresh green chilli, seeded and finely chopped
30 ml/2 tbsp sesame seeds, to serve
115 g/4 oz/1 cup peanuts, to serve

FOR THE DRESSING
15 ml/1 tbsp dark soy sauce
15 ml/1 tbsp light soy sauce
15 ml/1 tbsp runny honey
15 ml/1 tbsp rice wine or dry sherry
15 ml/1 tbsp sesame oil

2 Drain the noodles, refresh in cold water, then drain again.

3 Mix the noodles with all of the prepared vegetables.

1 Preheat the oven to 200°C/400°F/Gas 6. Cook the egg noodles in boiling water, following the instructions on the side of the packet.

celeriac
beansprouts
green chilli
spring onion
sesame seeds
water chestnuts
cucumber
carrot
peanuts
noodles

4 Combine the dressing ingredients in a small bowl, then toss into the noodle and vegetable mixture. Divide the salad between 4 plates.

5 Place the sesame seeds and peanuts on separate baking trays and place in the oven. Take the sesame seeds out after 5 minutes and continue to cook the peanuts for a further 5 minutes until evenly browned.

6 Sprinkle the sesame seeds and peanuts evenly over each portion and serve at once.

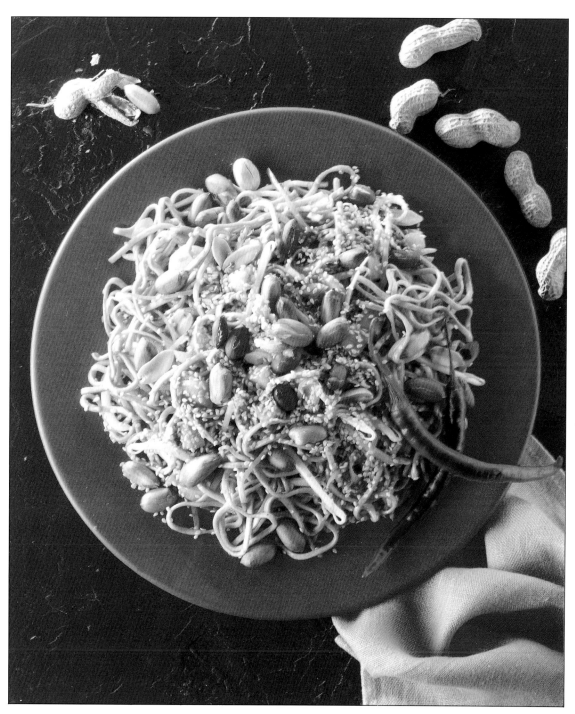

Penne with Aubergine and Mint Pesto

This splendid variation on the classic Italian pesto uses fresh mint rather than basil for a different flavour.

Serves 4

INGREDIENTS
2 large aubergines
salt
450 g/1 lb penne
50 g/2 oz walnut halves

FOR THE PESTO
25 g/1 oz fresh mint
15 g/½ oz flat-leaf parsley
40 g/1½ oz walnuts
40 g/1½ oz Parmesan cheese, finely
    grated
2 garlic cloves
90 ml/6 tbsp olive oil
salt and freshly ground black pepper

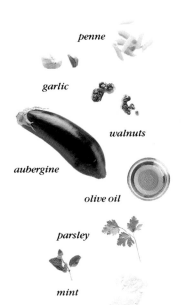

penne

garlic

walnuts

aubergine

olive oil

parsley

mint

Parmesan

1 Cut the aubergines lengthwise into 1 cm/½ in slices.

2 Cut the slices again crossways to give short strips.

3 Layer the strips in a colander with salt and leave to stand for 30 minutes over a plate to catch any juices. Rinse well in cool water and drain.

4 Place all the pesto ingredients, except the oil in a blender or food processor, blend until smooth, then gradually add the oil in a thin stream until the mixture amalgamates. Season to taste.

5 Cook the penne following the instructions on the side of the packet for about 8 minutes or until nearly cooked. Add the aubergine and cook for a further 3 minutes.

6 Drain well and mix in the mint pesto and walnut halves. Serve immediately.

Campanelle with Yellow Pepper Sauce

Roasted yellow peppers make a deliciously sweet and creamy sauce to serve with pasta.

Serves 4

INGREDIENTS
2 yellow peppers
50 g/2 oz/¼ cup soft goat's cheese
115 g/4 oz/½ cup low-fat fromage blanc
salt and freshly ground black pepper
450 g/1 lb short pasta such as campanelle or fusilli
50 g/2 oz/¼ cup flaked almonds, toasted, to serve

pepper

fromage blanc

flaked almonds

goat's cheese

campanelle

1 Place the whole yellow peppers under a preheated grill until charred and blistered. Place in a plastic bag to cool. Peel and remove the seeds.

2 Place the pepper flesh in a blender with the goat's cheese and fromage blanc. Blend until smooth. Season with salt and lots of black pepper.

3 Cook the pasta following the instructions on the side of the packet until *al dente*. Drain well.

4 Toss with the sauce and serve sprinkled with the toasted flaked almonds.

Spaghetti with Black Olive and Mushroom Sauce

A rich pungent sauce topped with sweet cherry tomatoes.

Serves 4

INGREDIENTS

15 ml/1 tbsp olive oil
1 garlic clove, chopped
225 g/8 oz mushrooms, chopped
150 g/5 oz/generous ½ cup black olives, pitted
30 ml/2 tbsp chopped fresh parsley
1 fresh red chilli, seeded and chopped
450 g/1 lb spaghetti
225 g/8 oz cherry tomatoes
slivers of Parmesan cheese, to serve (optional)

garlic

mushrooms

red chillies

cherry tomatoes

black olives

spaghetti

parsley

1 Heat the oil in a large pan. Add the garlic and cook for 1 minute. Add the mushrooms, cover, and cook over a medium heat for 5 minutes.

2 Place the mushrooms in a blender or food processor with the olives, parsley and red chilli. Blend until smooth.

3 Cook the pasta following the instructions on the side of the packet until *al dente*. Drain well and return to the pan. Add the olive mixture and toss together until the pasta is well coated. Cover and keep warm.

4 Heat an ungreased frying pan and shake the cherry tomatoes around until they start to split (about 2–3 minutes). Serve the pasta topped with the tomatoes and garnished with slivers of Parmesan, if liked.

Tagliatelle with Pea Sauce, Asparagus and Broad Beans

A creamy pea sauce makes a wonderful combination with the crunchy young vegetables.

Serves 4

INGREDIENTS
15 ml/1 tbsp olive oil
1 garlic clove, crushed
6 spring onions, sliced
225 g/8 oz/1 cup frozen peas,
   defrosted
350 g/12 oz fresh young asparagus
30 ml/2 tbsp chopped fresh sage, plus
extra leaves to garnish
finely grated rind of 2 lemons
450 ml/¾ pint/1¾ cups vegetable
   stock or water
225 g/8 oz frozen broad beans,
   defrosted
450 g/1 lb tagliatelle
60 ml/4 tbsp low-fat yogurt

lemon

garlic

asparagus

broad beans

peas

yogurt *tagliatelle*

sage

spring onion

1 Heat the oil in a pan. Add the garlic and spring onions and cook gently for 2–3 minutes until softened.

2 Add the peas and ⅓ of the asparagus, together with the sage, lemon rind and stock or water. Bring to the boil, reduce the heat and simmer for 10 minutes until tender. Purée in a blender until smooth.

3 Meanwhile remove the outer skins from the broad beans and discard.

4 Cut the remaining asparagus into 5 cm/2 in lengths trimming off any tough fibrous stems, and blanch in boiling water for 2 minutes.

5 Cook the tagliatelle following the instructions on the side of the packet until *al dente*. Drain well.

COOK'S TIP
Frozen peas and beans have been used here to cut down the preparation time, but the dish tastes even better if you use fresh young vegetables when in season.

6 Add the cooked asparagus and shelled beans to the sauce and reheat. Stir in the yogurt and toss into the tagliatelle. Garnish with a few extra sage leaves and serve.

Coriander Ravioli with Pumpkin filling

A stunning herb pasta with a superb creamy pumpkin and roast garlic filling.

Serves 4–6

INGREDIENTS
200 g/7 oz/scant 1 cup strong
    unbleached white flour
2 eggs
pinch of salt
45 ml/3 tbsp chopped fresh coriander
coriander sprigs, to garnish

FOR THE FILLING
4 garlic cloves in their skins
450 g/1 lb pumpkin, peeled and seeds
    removed
115 g/4 oz/½ cup ricotta
4 halves sun-dried tomatoes in olive
    oil, drained and finely chopped, but
    reserve 30 ml/2 tbsp of the oil
freshly ground black pepper

1 Place the flour, eggs, salt and coriander into a food processor. Pulse until combined.

2 Place the dough on a lightly floured board and knead well for 5 minutes, until smooth. Wrap in clear film and leave to rest in the fridge for 20 minutes.

3 Preheat the oven to 200°C/400°F/ Gas 6. Place the garlic cloves on a baking sheet and bake for 10 minutes until softened. Steam the pumpkin for 5–8 minutes until tender and drain well. Peel the garlic cloves and mash into the pumpkin together with the ricotta and drained sun-dried tomatoes. Season with black pepper.

coriander

egg

pumpkin

garlic

flour

ricotta

sun-dried tomatoes

4 Divide the pasta into 4 pieces and flatten slightly. Using a pasta machine, on its thinnest setting, roll out each piece. Leave the sheets of pasta on a clean tea-towel until slightly dried.

5 Using a 7.5 cm/3 in crinkle-edged round cutter, stamp out 36 rounds.

6 Top 18 of the rounds with a teaspoonful of mixture, brush the edges with water and place another round of pasta on top. Press firmly around the edges to seal. Bring a large pan of water to the boil, add the ravioli and cook for 3–4 minutes. Drain well and toss into the reserved tomato oil. Serve garnished with coriander sprigs.

Capellini with Rocket, Mange-tout and Pine Nuts

A light but filling pasta dish with the added pepperiness of fresh rocket.

Serves 4

INGREDIENTS
250 g/9 oz capellini or angel-hair pasta
225 g/8 oz mange-tout
175 g/6 oz rocket
50 g/2 oz/¼ cup pine nuts, roasted
30 ml/2 tbsp Parmesan cheese, finely
  grated (optional)
30 ml/2 tbsp olive oil (optional)

rocket

Parmesan

pine nuts

capellini

mange-tout

1 Cook the capellini or angel-hair pasta following the instructions on the side of the packet until *al dente*.

2 Meanwhile, carefully top and tail the mange-tout.

COOK'S TIP

Olive oil and Parmesan are optional as they obviously raise the fat content.

3 As soon as the pasta is cooked, drop in the rocket and mange-tout. Drain immediately.

4 Toss the pasta with the roasted pine nuts, and Parmesan and olive oil if using. Serve at once.

Pasta Bows with Fennel and Walnut Sauce

A scrumptious blend of walnuts and crisp steamed fennel.

Serves 4

INGREDIENTS

75 g/3 oz/½ cup walnuts, roughly chopped
1 garlic clove
25 g/1 oz fresh flat-leaf parsley, picked from the stalks
115 g/4 oz/½ cup ricotta cheese
450 g/1 lb pasta bows
450 g/1 lb fennel bulbs
chopped walnuts, to garnish

garlic

pasta bows

ricotta

fennel

parsley

walnut halves

chopped walnuts

1 Place the chopped walnuts, garlic and parsley in a food processor. Pulse until roughly chopped. Transfer to a bowl and stir in the ricotta.

2 Cook the pasta following the instructions on the side of the packet until *al dente*. Drain well.

3 Slice the fennel thinly and steam for 4–5 minutes until just tender but still crisp.

4 Return the pasta to the pan and add the walnut mixture and the fennel. Toss well and sprinkle with the chopped walnuts. Serve immediately.

Spring Vegetable Stir-fry

A colourful, dazzling medley of fresh and sweet young vegetables.

Serves 4

INGREDIENTS
15 ml/1 tbsp peanut oil
1 garlic clove, sliced
2.5 cm/1 in piece of fresh ginger root, finely chopped
115 g/4 oz baby carrots
115 g/4 oz patty pan squash
115 g/4 oz baby sweetcorn
115 g/4 oz French beans, topped and tailed
115 g/4 oz sugar-snap peas, topped and tailed
115 g/4 oz young asparagus, cut into 7.5 cm/3 in pieces
8 spring onions, trimmed and cut into 5 cm/2 in pieces
115 g/4 oz cherry tomatoes

FOR THE DRESSING
juice of 2 limes
15 ml/1 tbsp runny honey
15 ml/1 tbsp soy sauce
5 ml/1 tsp sesame oil

1 Heat the peanut oil in a wok or large frying pan.

2 Add the garlic and ginger and stir-fry over a high heat for 1 minute.

3 Add the carrots, patty pan squash, sweetcorn and beans and stir-fry for another 3–4 minutes.

4 Add the sugar-snap peas, asparagus, spring onions and cherry tomatoes and stir-fry for a further 1–2 minutes.

spring onion
sugar-snap peas
asparagus
baby sweetcorn
lime
patty pan squash
cherry tomatoes
carrot
ginger
garlic
French beans

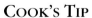 Mix the dressing ingredients together and add to the pan.

6 Stir well then cover the pan. Cook for 2–3 minutes more until the vegetables are just tender but still crisp.

COOK'S TIP
Stir-fries take only moments to cook so prepare this dish at the last minute.

Spinach and Potato Galette

Creamy layers of potato, spinach and herbs make a
warming supper dish.

Serves 6

INGREDIENTS
900 g/2 lb large potatoes
450 g/1 lb fresh spinach
2 eggs
400 g/14 oz/1¾ cup low-fat cream
    cheese
15 ml/1 tbsp grainy mustard
50 g/2 oz chopped fresh herbs
    (e.g. chives, parsley, chervil or
    sorrel)
salt and freshly ground black pepper

mustard

parsley

*cream
cheese*

spinach

egg   *potatoes*

chives

cherry tomatoes

chervil

sorrel

1 Preheat the oven to 180°C/350°F/
Gas 4. Line a deep 23 cm/9 in cake tin
with non-stick baking paper. Place the
potatoes in a large pan and cover with
cold water. Bring to the boil and cook for
10 minutes. Drain well and allow to cool
slightly before slicing thinly.

2 Wash the spinach and place in a large
pan with only the water that is clinging to
the leaves. Cover and cook, stirring once,
until the spinach has just wilted. Drain well
in a sieve and squeeze out the excess
moisture. Chop finely.

3 Beat the eggs with the cream cheese
and mustard then stir in the chopped
spinach and fresh herbs.

4 Place a layer of the sliced potatoes in
the lined tin, arranging them in concentric
circles. Top with a spoonful of the cream
cheese mixture and spread out. Continue
layering, seasoning with salt and pepper as
you go, until all the potatoes and the
cream cheese mixture are used up.

5 Cover the tin with a piece of foil and
place in a roasting tin.

6 Fill the roasting tin with enough
boiling water to come halfway up the
sides, and cook in the oven for 45–50
minutes. Turn out onto a plate and serve
hot or cold.

COOK'S TIP

Choose firm potatoes for this dish
such as Cara, Desirée or Estima.

Grilled Mixed Peppers with Feta and Green Salsa

Soft smoky grilled peppers make a lovely combination with the slightly tart salsa.

Serves 4

INGREDIENTS
4 medium peppers in different
   colours
45 ml/3 tbsp chopped fresh flat-leaf
   parsley
45 ml/3 tbsp chopped fresh dill
45 ml/3 tbsp chopped fresh mint
½ small red onion, finely chopped
15 ml/1 tbsp capers, coarsely chopped
50 g/2 oz/¼ cup Greek olives, pitted
   and sliced
1 fresh green chilli, seeded and finely
   chopped
60 g/4 tbsp pistachios, chopped
75 ml/5 tbsp extra-virgin olive oil
45 ml/3 tbsp fresh lime juice
115 g/4 oz/½ cup medium-fat feta
   cheese, crumbled
25 g/1 oz gherkins, finely chopped

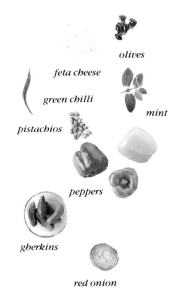

olives

feta cheese

green chilli

mint

pistachios

peppers

gherkins

red onion

1 Preheat the grill. Place the whole peppers on a tray and grill until charred and blistered.

2 Place the peppers in a plastic bag and leave to cool.

3 Peel, seed and cut the peppers into even strips.

4 Mix all the remaining ingredients together, and stir in the pepper strips.

COOK'S TIP
Feta cheese is quite salty so if preferred, soak in cold water and drain well before using.

Beetroot and Celeriac Gratin

Beautiful ruby-red slices of beetroot and celeriac make a stunning light accompaniment to any main course dish.

Serves 6

INGREDIENTS
350 g/12 oz raw beetroot
350 g/12 oz celeriac
4 thyme sprigs
6 juniper berries, crushed
salt and freshly ground black pepper
100 ml/4 fl oz/½ cup fresh orange
   juice
100 ml/4 fl oz/½ cup vegetable stock

celeriac

orange juice

juniper berries

beetroot

thyme

1 Preheat the oven to 190°C/375°F/ Gas 5. Peel and slice the beetroot very finely. Quarter and peel the celeriac and slice very finely.

2 Fill a 25 cm/10 in diameter, cast iron, ovenproof or flameproof frying pan with alternate layers of beetroot and celeriac slices, sprinkling with the thyme, juniper and seasoning between each layer.

3 Mix the orange juice and stock together and pour over the gratin. Place over a medium heat and bring to the boil. Boil for 2 minutes.

4 Cover with foil and place in the oven for 15–20 minutes. Remove the foil and raise the oven temperature to 200°C/ 400°F/Gas 6. Cook for a further 10 minutes.

Aubergine, Roast Garlic and Red Pepper Pâté

This is a simple pâté of smoky baked aubergine, sweet pink peppercorns and red peppers, with more than a hint of garlic!

Serves 4

INGREDIENTS
3 medium aubergines
2 red peppers
5 whole garlic cloves
7.5 ml/1½ tsp pink peppercorns in
  brine, drained and crushed
30 ml/2 tbsp chopped fresh coriander

aubergine

garlic

coriander

pink peppercorns

red pepper

1 Preheat the oven to 200°C/400°F/ Gas 6. Arrange the whole aubergines, peppers and garlic cloves on a baking sheet and place in the oven. After 10 minutes remove the garlic cloves and turn over the aubergines and peppers.

2 Peel the garlic cloves and place in the bowl of a blender.

3 After a further 20 minutes remove the blistered and charred peppers from the oven and place in a plastic bag. Leave to cool.

4 After a further 10 minutes remove the aubergines from the oven. Split in half and scoop the flesh into a sieve placed over a bowl. Press the flesh with a spoon to remove the bitter juices.

5 Add the mixture to the garlic in the blender and blend until smooth. Place in a large mixing bowl.

6 Peel and chop the red peppers and stir into the aubergine mixture. Mix in the peppercorns and fresh coriander and serve at once.

Courgettes and Asparagus en Papillote

An impressive dinner party accompaniment, these puffed paper parcels should be broken open at the table by each guest, so that the wonderful aroma can be fully appreciated.

Serves 4

INGREDIENTS
2 medium courgettes
1 medium leek
225 g/8 oz young asparagus, trimmed
4 tarragon sprigs
4 whole garlic cloves, unpeeled
salt and freshly ground black pepper
1 egg, beaten

courgettes

asparagus

leek

egg

tarragon

garlic

1 Preheat the oven to 200°C/400°F/ Gas 6. Using a potato peeler slice the courgettes lengthwise into thin strips.

2 Cut the leek into very fine julienne strips and cut the asparagus evenly into 5 cm/2 in lengths.

3 Cut out 4 sheets of greaseproof paper measuring 30 × 38 cm/12 × 15 in and fold in half. Draw a large curve to make a heart shape when unfolded. Cut along the inside of the line and open out.

4 Divide the courgettes, asparagus and leek evenly between each paper heart, positioning the filling on one side of the fold line, and topping each with a sprig of tarragon and an unpeeled garlic clove. Season to taste.

COOK'S TIP

Experiment with other vegetables and herbs such as sugar-snap peas and mint or baby carrots and rosemary. The possibilities are endless.

5 Brush the edges lightly with the beaten egg and fold over.

6 Pleat the edges together so that each parcel is completely sealed. Lay the parcels on a baking tray and cook for 10 minutes. Serve immediately.

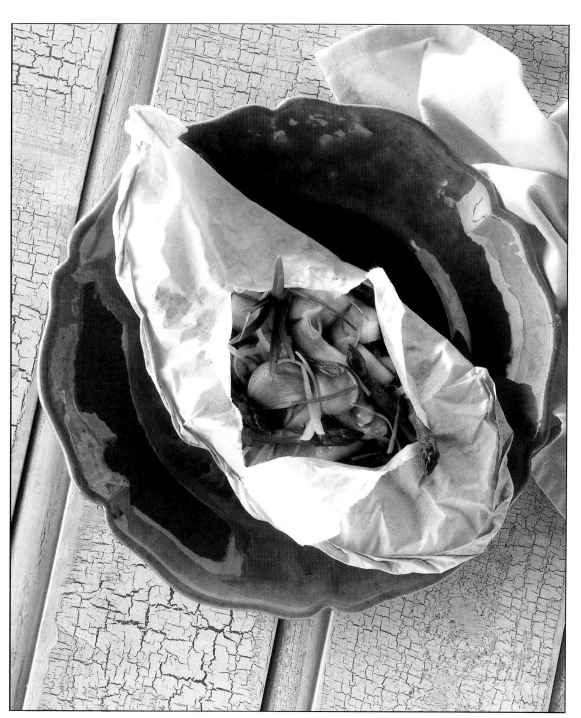

Broccoli and Chestnut Terrine

Served hot or cold, this versatile terrine is equally suitable for a dinner party as for a picnic.

Serves 4–6

INGREDIENTS

450 g/1 lb broccoli, cut into small florets
225 g/8 oz cooked chestnuts, roughly chopped
50 g/2 oz/1 cup fresh wholemeal breadcrumbs
60 ml/4 tbsp low-fat natural yogurt
30 ml/2 tbsp Parmesan cheese, finely grated
salt, grated nutmeg and freshly ground black pepper
2 eggs, beaten

yogurt

breadcrumbs

broccoli

chestnuts

egg

Parmesan

1 Preheat the oven to 180°C/350°F/Gas 4. Line a 900 g/2 lb loaf tin with non-stick baking paper.

2 Blanch or steam the broccoli for 3–4 minutes until just tender. Drain well. Reserve ¼ of the smallest florets and chop the rest finely.

3 Mix together the chestnuts, breadcrumbs, yogurt and Parmesan, and season to taste.

4 Fold in the chopped broccoli, reserved florets and the beaten eggs.

5 Spoon the broccoli mixture into the prepared tin.

6 Place in a roasting tin and pour in boiling water to come halfway up the sides of the loaf tin. Bake for 20–25 minutes. Remove from the oven and tip out onto a plate or tray. Serve cut into even slices.

Baked Squash

A creamy, sweet and nutty filling makes the perfect topping for tender buttery squash.

Serves 4

INGREDIENTS

2 butternut or acorn squash, 500 g/
   1¼ lb each
15 ml/1 tbsp olive oil
175 g/6 oz/¾ cup canned sweetcorn
   kernels, drained
115 g/4 oz/½ cup unsweetened
   chestnut purée
75 ml/5 tbsp low-fat yogurt
salt and freshly ground black pepper
50 g/2 oz/¼ cup fresh goat's cheese
snipped chives, to garnish

yogurt

chestnut purée

sweetcorn

butternut squash

goat's cheese

1 Preheat the oven to 180°C/350°F/ Gas 4. Cut the squash in half lengthwise.

2 Scoop out the seeds with a spoon and discard.

3 Place the squash halves on a baking sheet and brush the flesh lightly with the oil. Bake in the oven for 30 minutes.

4 Mix together the sweetcorn, chestnut purée and yogurt in a bowl. Season to taste.

5 Remove the squash from the oven and divide the chestnut mixture between them, spooning it into the hollows.

COOK'S TIP

Use mozzarella or other mild, soft cheeses in place of goat's cheese. The cheese can be omitted entirely for a lower-fat alternative.

6 Top each half with ¼ of the goat's cheese and return to the oven for a further 10–15 minutes. Garnish with snipped chives.

Red Cabbage in Port and Red Wine

A sweet and sour, spicy red cabbage dish, with the added crunch of pears and walnuts.

Serves 6

INGREDIENTS
15 ml/1 tbsp walnut oil
1 onion, sliced
2 whole star anise
5 ml/1 tsp ground cinnamon
pinch of ground cloves
450 g/1 lb red cabbage, finely
    shredded
25 g/1 oz/2 tbsp dark brown sugar
45 ml/3 tbsp red wine vinegar
300 ml/½ pint/1¼ cups red wine
150 ml/¼ pint/⅔ cup port
2 pears, cut into 1 cm/½ in cubes
115 g/4 oz/½ cup raisins
salt and freshly ground black pepper
115 g/4 oz/½ cup walnut halves

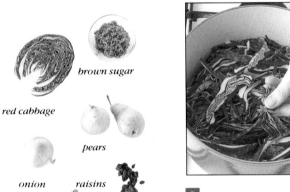

brown sugar

red cabbage

pears

onion   raisins

walnut halves

star anise

port

red wine vinegar

red wine

1 Heat the oil in a large pan. Add the onion and cook gently for about 5 minutes until softened.

2 Add the star anise, cinnamon, cloves and cabbage and cook for about 3 minutes more.

3 Stir in the sugar, vinegar, red wine and port. Cover the pan and simmer gently for 10 minutes, stirring occasionally.

4 Stir in the cubed pears and raisins and cook for a further 10 minutes or until the cabbage is tender. Season to taste. Mix in the walnut halves and serve.

Leek and Caraway Gratin with a Carrot Crust

Tender leeks are mixed with a creamy caraway sauce and a crunchy carrot topping.

Serves 4–6

INGREDIENTS

675 g/1½ lb leeks, cut into 5 cm/2 in pieces
150 ml/¼ pint/⅔ cup vegetable stock or water
45 ml/3 tbsp dry white wine
5 ml/1 tsp caraway seeds
pinch of salt
275 ml/10 fl oz skimmed milk as required
25 g/1 oz/2 tbsp butter
25 g/1 oz/¼ cup plain flour

FOR THE TOPPING

115 g/4 oz/2 cups fresh wholemeal breadcrumbs
115 g/4 oz/2 cups grated carrot
30 ml/2 tbsp chopped fresh parsley
75 g/3 oz Jarlsberg cheese, coarsely grated
25 g/1 oz/2 tbsp slivered almonds

parsley

vegetable stock

Jarlsberg

leek

breadcrumbs

butter

1 Place the leeks in a large pan. Add the stock or water, wine, caraway seeds and salt. Bring to a simmer, cover and cook for 5–7 minutes until the leeks are just tender.

2 With a slotted spoon, transfer the leeks to an ovenproof dish. Reduce the remaining liquid to half then make the amount up to 350 ml/12 fl oz/1 ½ cups with skimmed milk.

3 Preheat the oven to 180°C/350°F/ Gas 4. Melt the butter in a saucepan, stir in the flour and cook without allowing it to colour for 1–2 minutes. Gradually add the stock and milk, stirring well after each addition, until you have a smooth sauce. Simmer for 5–6 minutes then pour over the leeks in the dish.

4 Mix all the topping ingredients together in a bowl and sprinkle over the leeks. Bake for 20–25 minutes until golden.

Mushroom and Okra Curry with Fresh Mango Relish

This simple but delicious curry with its fresh gingery mango relish is best served with plain basmati rice.

Serves 4

INGREDIENTS
4 garlic cloves, roughly chopped
2.5 cm/1 in piece of fresh ginger root, peeled and roughly chopped
1–2 red chillies, seeded and chopped
175 ml/6 fl oz/¾ cup cold water
15 ml/1 tbsp sunflower oil
5 ml/1 tsp coriander seeds
5 ml/1 tsp cumin seeds
5 ml/1 tsp ground cumin
2 green cardamom pods, seeds removed and ground
pinch of ground turmeric
1 × 400 g/14 oz can chopped tomatoes
450 g/1 lb mushrooms, quartered if large
225 g/8 oz okra, trimmed and cut into 1 cm/½ in slices
30 ml/2 tbsp chopped fresh coriander
basmati rice, to serve

FOR THE MANGO RELISH
1 large ripe mango, about 500 g/1¼ lb in weight
1 small garlic clove, crushed
1 onion, finely chopped
10 ml/2 tsp grated fresh ginger root
1 fresh red chilli, seeded and finely chopped
pinch of salt and sugar

mango
onion
garlic
ginger
cumin seeds
mushrooms
okra
red chillies
chopped tomatoes
coriander seeds
turmeric
cardamom pods

1 For the mango relish, peel the mango and cut off the flesh from the stone.

2 In a bowl mash the mango flesh with a fork or pulse in a food processor, and mix in the rest of the relish ingredients. Set to one side.

3 Place the garlic, ginger, chilli and 45 ml/3 tbsp of the water into a blender and blend until smooth.

4 Heat the sunflower oil in a large pan. Add the whole coriander and cumin seeds and allow them to sizzle for a few seconds. Add the ground cumin, ground cardamom and turmeric and cook for 1 minute more.

5 Add the paste from the blender, the tomatoes, remaining water, mushrooms and okra. Stir to mix well and bring to the boil. Reduce the heat, cover, and simmer for 5 minutes.

6 Remove the cover, turn up the heat slightly and cook for another 5–10 minutes until the okra is tender. Stir in the fresh coriander and serve with rice and the mango relish.

Potato Gnocchi with Hazelnut Sauce

These delicate potato dumplings are dressed with a creamy hazelnut sauce.

Serves 4

INGREDIENTS
675 g/1½ lb large potatoes
115 g/4 oz/1 cup plain flour

FOR THE HAZELNUT SAUCE
115 g/4 oz/½ cup hazelnuts, roasted
1 garlic clove, roughly chopped
½ tsp grated lemon rind
½ tsp lemon juice
30 ml/2 tbsp sunflower oil
150 g/5 oz/scant ¾ cup low-fat
   fromage blanc
salt and freshly ground black pepper

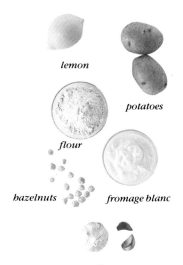

lemon

potatoes

flour

hazelnuts

fromage blanc

garlic

1 Place 65 g/2½ oz of the hazelnuts in a blender with the garlic, grated lemon rind and juice. Blend until coarsely chopped. Gradually add the oil and blend until smooth. Spoon into a bowl and mix in the fromage blanc. Season to taste.

2 Place the potatoes in a pan of cold water. Bring to the boil and cook for 20–25 minutes. Drain well in a colander.

When cool, peel and purée the potatoes whilst still warm by passing them through a food mill into a bowl.

3 Add the flour a little at a time (you may not need all the flour as potatoes vary in texture). Stop adding flour when the mixture is smooth and slightly sticky. Add salt to taste.

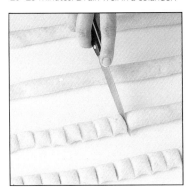

4 Roll out the mixture onto a floured board, into a long sausage about 1 cm/½ in in diameter. Cut into 2 cm/¾ in lengths.

5 Take 1 piece at a time and press it on to a floured fork. Roll each piece slightly while pressing it along the prongs and off the fork. Flip onto a floured plate or tray. Continue with the rest of the mixture.

COOK'S TIP
A light touch is the key to making soft gnocchi, so handle the dough as little as possible to prevent the mixture from becoming tough.

6 Bring a large pan of water to the boil and drop in 20–25 pieces at a time. They will rise to the surface very quickly. Let them cook for 10–15 seconds more, then lift them out with a slotted spoon. Drop into a dish and keep warm. Continue with the rest of the gnocchi. To heat the sauce, place in a heatproof bowl over a pan of simmering water and heat gently, being careful not to let the sauce curdle. Pour the sauce over the gnocchi. Roughly chop the remaining hazelnuts and scatter over the sauce.

Courgette and Walnut Loaf

Cardamom seeds impart their distinctive aroma to this loaf. Serve spread with ricotta and honey for a delicious snack.

Makes 1 loaf

INGREDIENTS

3 × size 3 eggs
75 g/3 oz/⅓ cup light muscovado
    sugar
100 ml/4 fl oz/½ cup sunflower oil
225 g/8 oz/2 cups wholemeal flour
5 ml/1 tsp baking powder
5 ml/1 tsp bicarbonate of soda
5 ml/1 tsp ground cinnamon
3 ml/¾ tsp ground allspice
7.5 ml/½ tbsp green cardamoms,
    seeds removed and crushed
150 g/5 oz courgette, coarsely grated
115 g/4 oz/½ cup walnuts, chopped
50 g/2 oz/¼ cup sunflower seeds

courgettes

egg

walnuts

sunflower oil

muscovado sugar

wholemeal flour

sunflower seeds

cardamom pods

1 Preheat the oven to 180°C/350°F/ Gas 4. Line the base and sides of a 900 g/ 2 lb loaf tin with non-stick baking paper.

2 Beat the eggs and sugar together and gradually add the oil.

3 Sift the flour into a bowl together with the baking powder, bicarbonate of soda, cinnamon and allspice.

4 Mix into the egg mixture with the rest of the ingredients, reserving 15 g/1 tbsp of the sunflower seeds for the top.

5 Spoon into the loaf tin, level off the top, and sprinkle with the reserved sunflower seeds.

6 Bake for 1 hour or until a skewer inserted in the centre comes out clean. Leave to cool slightly before turning out onto a wire rack to cool completely.

Red Pepper and Watercress Filo Parcels

Peppery watercress combines well with sweet red pepper in these crisp little parcels.

Makes 8

INGREDIENTS
3 red peppers
175 g/6 oz watercress
225 g/8 oz/1 cup ricotta cheese
50 g/2 oz/¼ cup blanched almonds,
 toasted and chopped
salt and freshly ground black pepper
8 sheets of filo pastry
30 ml/2 tbsp olive oil

ricotta

red pepper

watercress

almonds

filo pastry

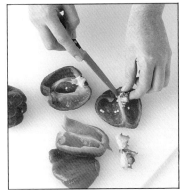

1 Preheat the oven to 190°C/375°F/ Gas 5. Place the peppers under a hot grill until blistered and charred. Place in a plastic bag. When cool enough to handle peel, seed and pat dry on kitchen paper.

2 Place the peppers and watercress in a food processor and pulse until coarsely chopped. Spoon into a bowl.

3 Mix in the ricotta and almonds, and season to taste.

4 Working with 1 sheet of filo pastry at a time, cut out 2 × 18 cm/7 in and 2 × 5 cm/2 in squares from each sheet. Brush 1 large square with a little olive oil and place a second large square at an angle of 90 degrees to form a star shape.

5 Place 1 of the small squares in the centre of the star shape, brush lightly with oil and top with a second small square.

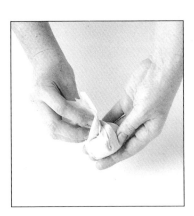

6 Top with ⅛ of the red pepper mixture. Bring the edges together to form a purse shape and twist to seal. Place on a lightly greased baking sheet and cook for 25–30 minutes until golden.

Sage Soda Bread

This wonderful loaf, quite unlike bread made with yeast, has a velvety texture and a powerful sage aroma.

Makes 1 loaf

INGREDIENTS
225 g/8 oz/2 cups wholemeal flour
115 g/4 oz/1 cup strong white flour
2.5 ml/½ tsp salt
5 ml/1 tsp bicarbonate of soda
30 ml/2 tbsp shredded fresh sage
300–450 ml/½–¾ pint/1¼–1¾
   cups buttermilk

white flour

wholemeal flour

sage

buttermilk

1 Preheat the oven to 220°C/425°F/ Gas 7. Sift the dry ingredients into a bowl.

COOK'S TIP
As an alternative to the sage, try using finely chopped rosemary or thyme.

2 Stir in the sage and add enough buttermilk to make a soft dough.

3 Shape the dough into a round loaf and place on a lightly oiled baking sheet.

4 Cut a deep cross in the top. Bake in the oven for 40 minutes until the loaf is well risen and sounds hollow when tapped on the bottom. Leave to cool on a wire rack.

Mini Pizzas

For a quick supper dish try these delicious little pizzas made with fresh and sun-dried tomatoes.

Makes 4

INGREDIENTS
1 × 150 g/5 oz packet pizza mix
8 halves sun-dried tomatoes in olive oil, drained
50 g/2 oz/½ cup black olives, pitted
225 g/8 oz ripe tomatoes, sliced
50 g/2 oz/¼ cup goat's cheese
30 ml/2 tbsp fresh basil leaves

basil

tomatoes

sun-dried tomatoes

black olives

goat's cheese

1 Preheat the oven to 200°C/400°F/ Gas 6. Make up the pizza base following the instructions on the side of the packet.

2 Divide the dough into 4 and roll each piece out to a 13 cm/5 in disc. Place on a lightly oiled baking sheet.

3 Place the sun-dried tomatoes and olives in a blender or food processor and blend until smooth. Spread the mixture evenly over the pizza bases.

4 Top with the tomato slices and crumble over the goat's cheese. Bake for 10–15 minutes. Sprinkle with the fresh basil and serve.

COOK'S TIP

You could use loose sun-dried tomatoes (preserved without oil) instead. Leave in a bowl of warm water for 10–15 minutes to soften, drain and blend with the olives.

Parsnip and Pecan Gougères with Watercress and Rocket Sauce

These scrumptious nutty puffs conceal a surprisingly sweet parsnip centre.

Makes 18

INGREDIENTS
115 g/4 oz/½ cup butter
300 ml/½ pint/1¼ cups water
75 g/3 oz/¾ cup plain flour
50 g/2 oz/½ cup wholemeal flour
3 × size 3 eggs, beaten
25 g/1 oz Cheddar cheese, grated
pinch of cayenne pepper or paprika
75 g/3 oz/⅔ cup pecans, chopped
1 medium parsnip, cut into
    18 × 2 cm/¾ in pieces
15 ml/1 tbsp skimmed milk
10 ml/2 tsp sesame seeds

FOR THE SAUCE
150 g/5 oz watercress, trimmed
150 g/5 oz rocket, trimmed
175 ml/6 fl oz/¾ cup low-fat yogurt
salt, grated nutmeg and freshly ground
    black pepper
watercress sprigs, to garnish

1 Preheat the oven to 200°C/400°F/ Gas 6. Place the butter and water in a pan. Bring to the boil and add all the flour in one go. Beat vigorously until the mixture leaves the sides of the pan and forms a ball. Remove from heat and allow the mixture to cool slightly. Beat in the eggs a little at a time until the mixture is shiny and soft enough to fall gently from a spoon.

2 Beat in the Cheddar, cayenne pepper or paprika and the chopped pecans.

pecans

Cheddar

parsnips

rocket

wholemeal flour

plain flour

egg

yogurt

watercress

3 Lightly grease a baking sheet and drop onto it 18 heaped tablespoons of the mixture. Place a piece of parsnip on each and top with another heaped tablespoon of the mixture.

4 Brush the gougères with a little milk and sprinkle with sesame seeds. Bake in the oven for 25–30 minutes until firm and golden.

5 Meanwhile make the sauce. Bring a pan of water to the boil and blanch the watercress and rocket for 2–3 minutes. Drain and immediately refresh in cold water. Drain well and chop.

6 Purée the watercress and rocket in a blender or food processor with the yogurt until smooth. Season to taste with salt, nutmeg and freshly ground black pepper. To reheat, place the sauce in a bowl over a gently simmering pan of hot water and heat gently, taking care not to let the sauce curdle. Garnish with watercress.

Tomato Breadsticks

Once you've tried this simple recipe you'll never buy manufactured breadsticks again. Serve with aperitifs with a dip or with cheese to end a meal.

Makes 16

INGREDIENTS
225 g/8 oz/2 cups plain flour
2.5 ml/½ tsp salt
7.5 ml/½ tbsp easy-blend dry yeast
5 ml/1 tsp honey
5 ml/1 tsp olive oil
150 ml/¼ pint/⅔ cup warm water
6 halves sun-dried tomatoes in olive oil, drained and chopped
15 ml/1 tbsp skimmed milk
10 ml/2 tsp poppy seeds

plain flour

sun-dried tomatoes

honey

yeast

poppy seeds

1 Place the flour, salt and yeast in a food processor. Add the honey and olive oil and, with the machine running, gradually pour in the water (you may not need it all as flours vary). Stop adding water as soon as the dough starts to cling together. Process for 1 minute more.

2 Turn out the dough onto a floured board and knead for 3–4 minutes until springy and smooth. Knead in the chopped sun-dried tomatoes. Form into a ball and place in a lightly oiled bowl. Leave to rise for 5 minutes.

3 Preheat the oven to 150°C/300°F/ Gas 2. Divide the dough into 16 pieces and roll each piece into a 28 cm × 1 cm/ 11 in × ½ in long stick. Place on a lightly oiled baking sheet and leave to rise in a warm place for 15 minutes.

4 Brush the sticks with milk and sprinkle with poppy seeds. Bake for 30 minutes. Leave to cool on a wire rack.

Oatmeal Tartlets with Minted Hummus

Serve these wholesome little tartlets with a crisp salad of cos lettuce.

Serves 6

INGREDIENTS

225 g/8 oz/1½ cups medium oatmeal
2.5 ml/½ tsp bicarbonate of soda
5 ml/1 tsp salt
25g/1 oz/2 tbsp butter
1 egg yolk
30 ml/2 tbsp skimmed milk
1 × 400 g/14 oz can chick-peas,
    rinsed and drained
juice of 1–2 lemons
350 g/12 oz/1½ cups low-fat fromage
    blanc
60 ml/4 tbsp tahini
freshly ground black pepper
45 ml/3 tbsp chopped fresh mint
25 g/1 oz/2 tbsp pumpkin seeds
paprika, for dusting

pumpkin seeds

tahini

fromage blanc

chick-peas

oatmeal

mint

lemon

1 Preheat the oven to 160°C/325°F/ Gas 3. Mix together the oatmeal, bicarbonate of soda and salt in a large bowl. Rub in the butter until the mixture resembles fine breadcrumbs. Stir in the egg yolk and add the milk if the mixture seems too dry.

2 Press into 6 × 9 cm/3½ in tartlet tins. Bake for 25–30 minutes. Allow to cool.

3 Purée the chick-peas, the juice of 1 lemon, fromage blanc and tahini in a food processor until smooth. Spoon into a bowl and season with black pepper and more lemon juice to taste. Stir in the chopped mint. Divide between the tartlet moulds, sprinkle with pumpkin seeds and dust with paprika.

Saffron Focaccia

A dazzling yellow bread that is light in texture and distinctive in flavour.

Makes 1 loaf

INGREDIENTS
pinch of saffron threads
150 ml/¼ pint/⅔ cup boiling water
225 g/8 oz/2 cups plain flour
2.5 ml/½ tsp salt
5 ml/1 tsp easy-blend dry yeast
15 ml/1 tbsp olive oil

FOR THE TOPPING
2 garlic cloves, sliced
1 red onion, cut into thin wedges
rosemary sprigs
12 black olives, pitted and coarsely
   chopped
15 ml/1 tbsp olive oil

flour

garlic

rosemary

red onion

olives

saffron

yeast

1 Place the saffron in a heatproof jug and pour on the boiling water. Leave to stand and infuse until lukewarm.

2 Place the flour, salt, yeast and olive oil in a food processor. Turn on and gradually add the saffron and its liquid. Process until the dough forms into a ball.

3 Turn onto a floured board and knead for 10–15 minutes. Place in a bowl, cover and leave to rise for 30–40 minutes until doubled in size.

4 Punch down the risen dough on a lightly floured surface and roll out into an oval shape, 1 cm/½ in thick. Place on a lightly greased baking tray and leave to rise for 20–30 minutes.

5 Preheat the oven to 200°C/400°F/ Gas 6. Use your fingers to press small indentations all over the surface of the focaccia.

6 Cover with the topping ingredients, brush lightly with olive oil, and bake for 25 minutes or until the loaf sounds hollow when tapped on the bottom. Leave to cool on a wire rack.

INDEX